REES, BEES AND B

AVE THE GUM TR

G BLUE SEAS SA

ES, BEES AND BIG

VE THE GUM TRE

BLUE SEAS SAV

EES, BEES AND BI

THE GUM TR

M TREES, BEES A

SAVE THE GUM TREES, BEES AND BIG BLUE SEAS

LUKE JOHN
MATTHEW ARNOLD

A Scholastic Press book from Scholastic Australia

To the little legends in my life,
Jackson, Isabel, Harrison, Max, Rosa and Orson.
Thank you for always looking after the
gum trees, bees and big blue seas.
Big love, Luke.

Scholastic Press
An imprint of Scholastic Australia Pty Limited
(ABN 11 000 614 577)
PO Box 579 Gosford NSW 2250
www.scholastic.com.au

Part of the Scholastic Group
Sydney • Auckland • New York • Toronto • London • Mexico City
New Delhi • Hong Kong • Buenos Aires • Puerto Rico

First published by Scholastic Australia in 2025.

A catalogue record for this book is available from the National Library of Australia

ISBN: 978-1-76026-497-0

Hand-lettered by Luke John Matthew Arnold.

The illustrations in this book were created digitally.
Book design by Hannah Janzen and Luke John Matthew Arnold.

With thanks to Uluṟu-Kata Tjuṯa National Park for permitting the inclusion of an illustration of Uluru on Aṉangu Pitjantjatjara Yankunytjatjara Country.

Scholastic Press, with Luke John Matthew Arnold, acknowledges the Traditional Owners of the Country on which we live and work. We pay respect to Elders past and present.

Printed in China by Toppan Leefung Printing Ltd.

Scholastic Australia's policy, in association with Toppan Leefung, is to use papers that are renewable and made efficiently with wood from responsibly managed sources, so as to minimise its environmental footprint.

10 9 8 7 6 5 4 3 2

26 27 28 29 / 2

AS OUR HOMES

GET BIGGER...

THE CITIES GET WIDER AND THE ROADS GET LONGER ...

WE HAVE TO PONDER
HOW WE CAN ...

SAVE THE GUM TREES,

BEES

AND BIG

BLUE SEAS.

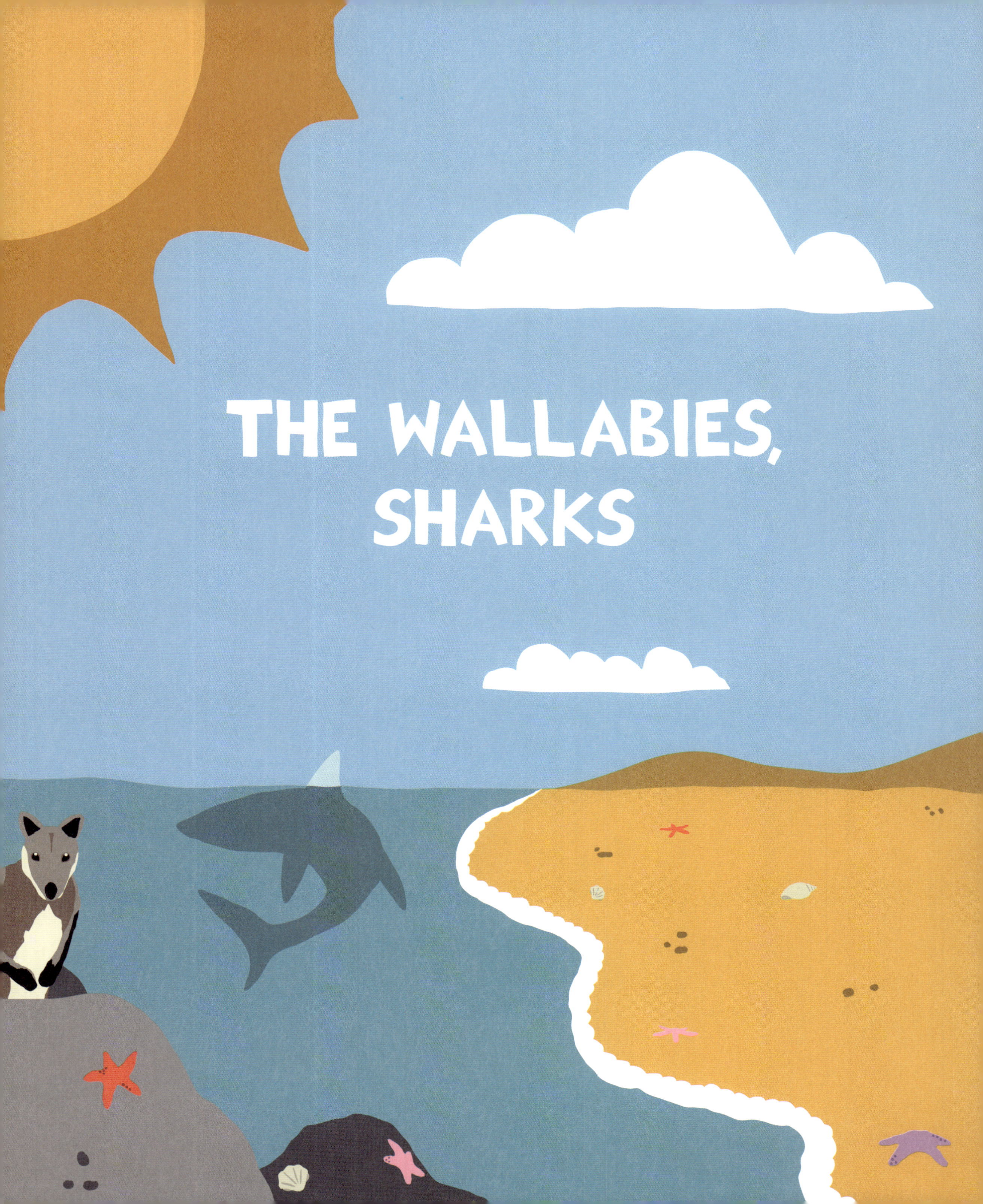
THE WALLABIES,
SHARKS

AND
NATIONAL PARKS.

THE KOALAS,
GALAHS

AND
WARATAHS.

THE EMUS, COCKATOOS

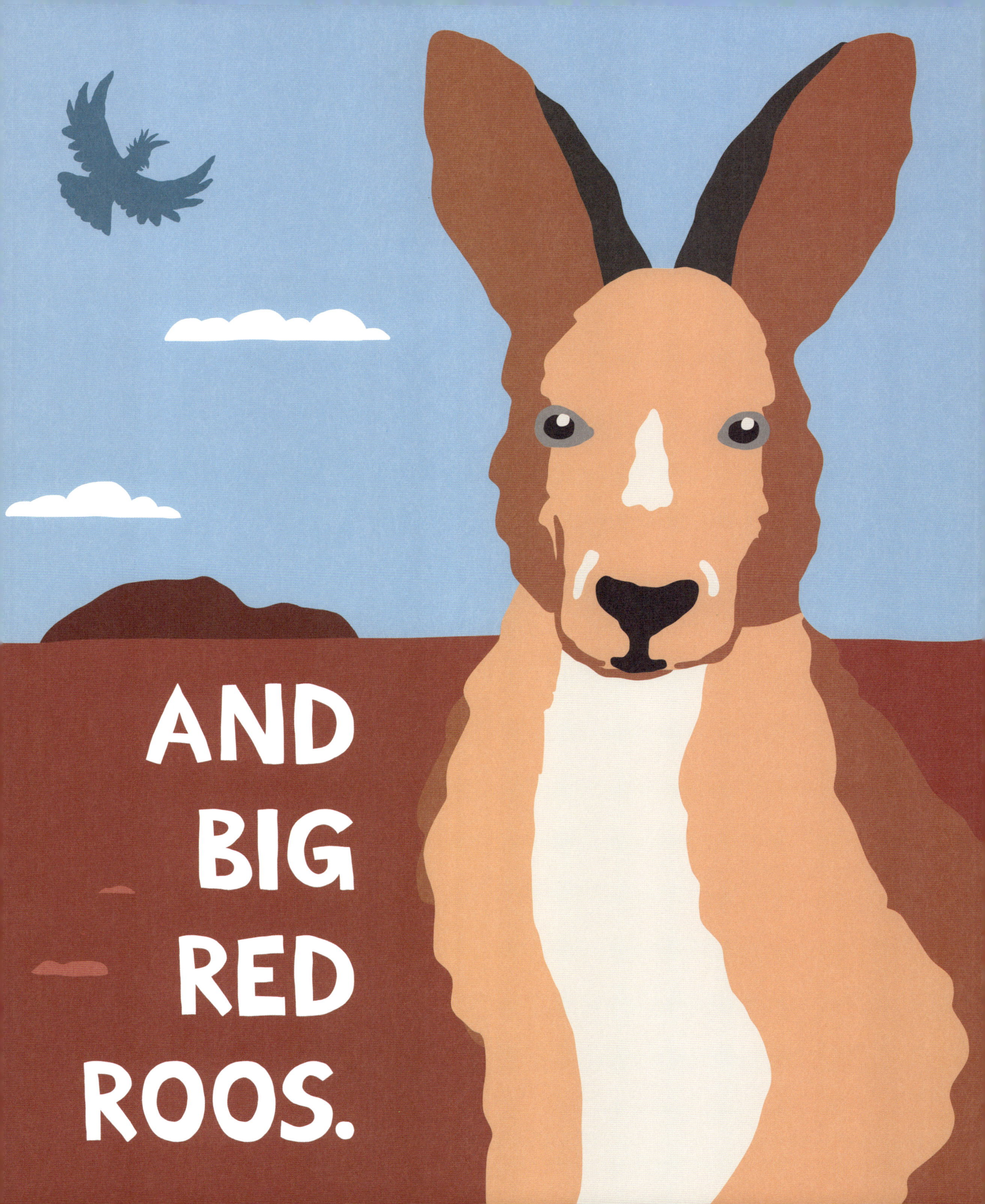
AND
BIG
RED
ROOS.

THE LIZARDS,

SANDS AND ...

SACRED

LANDS.

THE RIVERS, FLOWERS

AND OUR UNBREAKABLE POWER.

LET'S SAVE A SUNBURNT COUNTRY!

LET'S
MAKE OUR
HOMES GREENER,
THE CITIES
CLEANER,

THE ROADS SAFER, SO THERE'S A PLACE FOR ...

YOU, ME AND THE

BIG GUM TREES.

SAVE THE GUM T
BIG BLUE SEAS S
EES, BEES AND B
VE THE GUM TR
IG BLUE SEAS SA
ES, BEES AND BI
AVE THE GUM T
BLUE SEAS SAVE
EAS SAVE THE G